The Road of My Life

Ida Nikkel
(Humphrey) nee: Buchi

The Road of My Life

Copyright © 2017 by Ida Nikkel (Humphrey) nee: Buchi

No part of this publication may be reproduced, distributed, or transmitted in any form or by any means, including photocopying, recording, or other electronic or mechanical methods, without the prior written permission of the author, except in the case of brief quotations embodied in critical reviews and certain other non-commercial uses permitted by copyright law.

Tellwell Talent
www.tellwell.ca

ISBN
978-1-77302-640-4 (Paperback)

In The Beginning

My parents, Gus and Caroline Buchi, were newly married when they emigrated from Switzerland to Canada, and learning the English language was part of the experiences they faced. After a years' required indenture to a farmer in Cardale, Manitoba, they moved to Prince George, BC. My brother, Fred, was their first-born child, in 1924, and I was born next, in 1925. Now begins my story!

The Road of My Life • 3

Our parents' first home was a small two room shack my father built on McMillan Creek. We had a pair of goats for milk, and I remember fishing for creek trout. We had no neighbours, and the property was not adequate for farming, so Father bought 160 acres of bush-land in Fraser Flats, about 8 miles north of the city. Now there was land to clear! First, he built a simple log house, which had two small bedrooms, and the rest was open space. It was primitive but adequate. It was heated with a wood-burning stove made from a discarded oil barrel, to which was welded a metal door and legs. Fallen wood was sawn into blocks by hand. There were no chainsaws or splitters back then!

Fraser Flats was a close-knit community of six families, who farmed and worked at local sawmills. It was there I lived until I left home to work as a 'hired girl' on a farm, where I had my very first dish of cornflakes for breakfast. I loved it at first bite! We only had oatmeal porridge for breakfast, and to this day I never have it for breakfast! (In cookies, yes.) My first memory of punishment was when I gave the 50 pound cloth bag of sugar in the hall an angry shove. It tipped over and some of it spilled. This was a very serious mistake, as some things that could be grown, harvested and preserved required sugar, which was, as all other necessities, very precious. And to replace them meant an 8 mile trip to town by horse and wagon or sleigh. I was angry at my brother because I had to help him split firewood and carry it in to the wood box. I went into the bedroom to cry, and swore I would never stop! However, my mom couldn't stand that any longer. She came in, hugged me and apologized for striking me. Actually physical punishment was seldom used on us kids, as a 'look' from the parent was sufficient to produce the desired result from the errant kid!

My first Christmas that comes to memory was when I received the gift of a toothbrush in a celluloid case, which had been tucked under the log that supported the ceiling! The idea of Christmas only became a reality when I was of school age. We always had a Christmas concert, and all the neighbours came, as the one-roomed schoolhouse was our only public gathering place. It was cozy with a wood heater, but had no indoor plumbing. There was just an outhouse nearby. A collection was taken for the teacher to shop for candies, oranges, apples and nuts. Then one of the fathers, dressed in a Santa suit, would hand out bags of those treats to the children. One time it was our father, but we never guessed! After Santa was done, the small children and babies dozed and slept on quilts in a corner, and the adults danced to the music from a small gramophone one of the neighbours brought along.

Fraser Flats School

Winter was not an excuse to skip school, whatever the weather indicated, but I did skip barefooted at times on the first frozen ground, from sunny patch to sunny patch until the order of winter rubber boots from the Eaton's catalog arrived in town at the post office. If last winter's boots were too small, they were handed down to the next sibling. We looked forward to the parcels of hand-me-downs from a distant cousin in New York. That family had a girl a year older than I, and she wore clothes for only one season then they were mailed to my parents. Her summer dresses arrived the following spring for me to wear, and her winter clothes came in time for me to wear the following winter. This went on for several years then the families lost touch with each other.

Hand knitting socks was Mother's spare time duty. The socks were produced from yarn ordered also from the Eaton's mail order catalog. My mom taught me how to knit socks and mitts at an early age. After the first snowfall, if you had skis, you skied to school. The skis were leaned against the wall. At noon and recess we all dashed outside and fastened them onto our boots by placing a narrow rubber band (cut from old inner tubes) on a boot, tugging it over the 'toe-cap' in front, and around the heel at the back. This allowed for flexibility, but too much flexing made the band flip off into the snow and was often difficult to retrieve. My first pair of skis were made for me from birch wood by a neighbour, and they were beautiful! I skied to school, and when the bigger boys made a ski jump on the hillside by the school, I tried the jump, but I fell. I never tried that again. Sometimes there was a thaw then it got cold again, which produced a crust on the snow, sturdy enough for us to walk on. Of course there was also those softer places where the foot would break through, and the painful result was a scraped and bleeding leg!

When I was about eleven, my best friend was one of the neighbour's girls, Vera Saunderson. She and several of her older brothers were musically inclined, so at noon when the teacher would go to another of the neighbours, (the Youngs, I believe), for lunch, my friend would sing and hum. She and I would dance while the rest of the class was outside playing ball or tag or wrestling. Dancing was my greatest pleasure, and it still is! My first public dance later on was with her and her older brother who had a car by then. We drove to the local Farmers' Institute, a distance I had never travelled before, about 15 miles! A few of the neighbours were fortunate enough to own a car or truck; we were not!

My brother, Fred, was my role model. I was more 'boy' oriented than 'girl,' and when Uncle Walter gave him 25 cents for his birthday he spent it on a box of .22 rifle shells. He would be hunting for rabbits, grouse or any fur bearing animal to sell the pelt to the Hudson's Bay Company. They were eventually used by the air force pilots in WW2 to provide warmth in their helmets. The animal hides had to be scraped clean, stretched and mounted on a shaped board until they dried. I don't remember how I came to have 5 cents, but I talked Fred into selling me five shells and letting me borrow the gun to go hunting. Squirrels were plentiful and considered pests because of their propensity to chew their way into any building that stored grain or seeds. I put my snowshoes on and headed for the bush with the gun. I soon located several trees that had squirrel tunnels, where the harvested cones were stored for the winter. I got four squirrels with my five bullets! Now I had to skin them and make my own stretcher boards. Fred refused to help me! He and I used to torment our younger brother, Ivor. That was easy, as he was three years younger, born in June 1929. One day when our parents had gone to town, we got him up on the roof of the woodshed, sat him on an old sheet and lowered him over the edge to swing him, but I lost my hold on the sheet, and he fell down into the grass and weeds. He was not wearing a diaper, so his bottom made contact with some nettles. I don't recall how we ever explained the rash!

Sometimes we slept in the hayloft and watched the barn swallows fly in and out, and sometimes mice would come close to our heads while they were looking for hayseeds! We loved fishing. The nearest creek contained small trout, and my brother was lucky enough to get a pocketknife as a present, so he cut lengths of willow, to which we attached string and a bent pin for a hook! The bait was either a small gob of dough or a bug found under a rock or in the grass. In the Fraser River sometimes we used a ling line, which was a longer length of sturdy string with a weight on the end and several shorter pieces of baited hooks along it. This main line was then anchored to the shore of the river, and the end was flung out into the water, where we would leave it overnight and check on it the next morning. Sometimes there was no fish, sometimes two or three. The best catch we got was a lingcod that we carried home by putting a stick through its mouth and then on our shoulders with its tail dragging on the ground! (They are apparently a burbot.) The river was not only a place to fish. More than one neighbour who lived close to it used it for transportation to go to town by motor boat in the summer. It was faster and easier than going by horse and wagon. When I was about ten years old, my dad's cousin, Albert, and his wife, Cora, who lived a short walk from the river, asked me to babysit their children while they went to town by boat to go shopping. I was relieved when they came home safely, four hours later!

The river usually froze over in winter, so shopping trips to town in winter were cold and dangerous and avoided as much as possible. Sleigh rides were not the fun and cozy ones that Santa makes. They were made more endurable by heating a rock or brick and tucking it in the seat of the sleigh. A memorable trip my brother and I made was to get our Eaton's winter clothing parcel. When the clerk handed it over the counter, we wondered if we could possibly carry it home! Leaving it was NOT an option! Because it was tied with heavy twine, we managed to carry it by each grasping a handhold and sharing the weight. We were so lucky to get a sleigh ride from a neighbour on his way home. With still a long two miles to go, it helped us a lot.

One summer trip to town by wagon took us to the 'feed shed' where the horses were tied and fed. It had a counter and bench where we could sit and eat lunch after the shopping was finished. The lunch was a real treat: a loaf of bakers' bread and a chunk of bologna! We always had our own butcher's knife with us, and butter was not necessary.

We sometimes visited with a family who had come from Europe as well, and kept in touch. They lived in town, and those children were not used to farm animals. Cows are curious creatures and would approach strangers to sniff and check them out. The children shrieked and ran away! We had one cow that my brother would try to ride!

Lady, Kitty, and Bird

Our horses were also for working, not riding, but later on another horse was purchased, a young one, which had not been trained yet. It was being 'broken in' to harness as well as a saddle, and one day I decided to ride it to visit a neighbour. I managed to get the saddle on, rode to the neighbours', loosened the girth, tied the horse to the water trough and had my visit. When I re-tightened the girth, untied the horse and put one foot in the stirrup and the other leg halfway over, the horse started to buck!

I flew over the horse's back and landed in the dirt but wasn't hurt. The horse took off at a gallop, the saddle hanging under its belly and me in pursuit! It headed through the bush to a neighbouring yard where I caught it and managed to get the saddle back up. I cinched it tight and made the beast gallop all the way home!

Regina and Jobs

When I was eleven, the local school had to close because there were not enough children attending to allow the teacher to be paid. So when a former neighbour offered to take me with him to Regina, Saskatchewan to go to school, my parents agreed. This man's home was on the outskirts of the city. He was an employee of the railroad and travelled on the rail for free. As a 'family member' I could travel on his pass. I learned within days of our arrival that I was going to earn my keep! The family consisted of father, mother and two teenaged boys. I had to sleep on the couch that winter, and the next spring on an old bed frame that was moved onto a sort of patio that was not much larger than the bed. I had no clothes closet or drawers, but I had very few clothes, anyway, so it didn't matter! I had no privacy at all. My days began with getting dressed, getting breakfast for the father, so he could go to work. Then I prepared breakfast for the boys. There was no cooking involved, just cereal, toast and milk. Then their mother would finally come downstairs for hers. By this time, the clock said 'get to school, or you'll be late!' On Mondays I had to stay home to do the laundry. On weekends it was time to scrub floors, bathroom and clean windows.

I was so homesick! I wrote a letter home and begged for an envelope and a 3 cent stamp, and since I didn't know where to mail the letter, I gave it to them to mail. I soon realized from their attitude that they had read my letter. So I wrote another one at school, made an envelope, took the cancelled stamp off an old envelope, glued it on my hand-made one, and walked until I found a letter box to toss it in! My parents couldn't raise the $15.00 a fare would cost. They tried to sell potatoes, but the grocer told them, "Eat them," so I had to stay. I did pass my grade 8 exam but with a couple of 'D's and one 'E'. I still have the report card! I was poor in math and had not taken any music classes or home economics classes in my country school up to grade 7.

That summer there was a grasshopper plague so severe that the trains couldn't move on the 'grasshopper- greased' tracks. They had to be sanded! The Mrs. had planted a small garden and covered a head of cabbage with a bucket, but when she checked, the whole cabbage head had been eaten by the 'hoppers!

There was one girl who befriended me. One winter day, she invited me out with a group of girls to go tobogganing. We had to take a bus to get to a hill suitable for tobogganing. It's very flat land around Regina. I had no money, had never been on a bus and didn't realize you had to pay a fare, so I just followed the girls on board. The driver said, "Somebody didn't pay. Who?" Nobody spoke up. He just glared, shrugged and drove off! We ended our trip when two of the toboggans piled up at the bottom of the hill, and one girl had a broken leg! I accepted an offer of a ride back when a father to one of the girls came to get her.

Finally, I travelled by train again back to Prince George. I was 'train-sick' nauseous nearly all the way. There was no warm greeting when I arrived safely home. I was just told I should not have gone in the first place! By then my sisters, Alice and Leona, had been born, and my two brothers were old enough to take care of the chores and 'men's' work,' so my mother could now easily manage the housework, not having to do farm labour.

So when one of the neighbours stopped by to ask if I would come to replace their hired girl, who was leaving to marry, I said "Yes." I packed my few clothes in a cloth bag and climbed up the bush trail that his two older children travelled on earlier when school was open. I arrived at my new 'home' and met the family.

Some of the Turner family

16 • Ida Nikkel (Humphrey) nee: Buchi

(See the Turners' story with Ida's pictures in the book, *From Broadaxe to Clay Chinking* by June Chamberland ISBN 0-921087-33-0) The father appeared to be an old man, the wife was less than half his age and of a different nationality. The children were Jimmie, seven years; Laura, six years; Ruthie, five years; Donnie, three years; and Eddie, 9 months. My day began with diapering and dressing the baby, supervising the others and making breakfast ready by the time milking was finished. Then I did the dishes, bed-making and general housework. It was never-ending work because the wife was what we could call today a 'clean freak,' and the house had no indoor plumbing or electricity! They had a hired man, who did most of the chores. He and the mother did the milking, as the father was unable to milk due to the fact that he had two missing fingers. The herd was the main revenue for the farm, as the milk was sold to the creamery in town. One morning this hired man left the trap door to the small cellar storage open. It was dark in the kitchen, and I stepped in and slid down 6 feet of stairs on my back. Luckily, I wasn't hurt.

I shared a double bed with the five and six year old girls. They were of school age, but there was no school close enough to attend, so a correspondence course was applied for from the province. The grade one paperwork arrived, and now I with my grade 8 diploma was a school teacher! These two pupils passed their grade one provincial exam with flying colours! One of the events during my time there was a 70th surprise birthday party the wife organized for her husband, complete with a two-piece band for dance music and a birthday cake. I decorated the cake with an aluminum tube decorator I purchased with part of my $8.00 a month salary. Then I got my first ever brand new dress to wear and a camera and film for $1.25! The camera was a 'baby brownie.' I loved it and took lots of pictures. I used it for years and still have some of the prints.

By now I wanted a change. So when a family acquaintance needed a housekeeper to look after the children while their mother went to hospital to give birth to another one, I took it on. They already had three children, a boy who was four years old, a girl three years old and another boy still in diapers! By the time the new baby was brought home, I had potty-trained the little boy, so we had only one baby in diapers. Back then we used cloth diapers that had to be washed by hand, unless you were rich or lucky enough to have a washing machine! We never even had tap water, only a well and a hand pump, or else a well with a bucket on a rope. Very soon the new mother was able to take over again, so now I had to find another job.

I was given an address in town where they needed someone for the same type of job that I had just finished. So I applied and was taken on. However, not intending to spend my life on temporary 'fill-in' jobs when I heard that one of the restaurants was looking for help, I applied and was hired. This job involved some kitchen work, peeling vegetables, washing dishes and setting tables but no waitressing. Along with the $20.00 a month salary was a shared room in an adjoining one-bedroom shack. I was able to save enough money to buy a second-hand bike, and spent every moment possible on this prized possession! I liked my fellow employee, the waitress. She had a truck driver boyfriend. One day the boss' sister told me I had to wash our bedding by hand because I hadn't remembered to bring it in on wash day. I stood before this woman and said loud and clear, "I will not!" because I didn't like her anyway. And I didn't have to be told I had no job as of then! I went out to the shack for my stuff, and that afternoon when the truck driver came to visit his girlfriend, he suggested I apply at another café located downtown. I immediately did and was hired to be their laundress! They had table linen, chefs' aprons and hats, and their bed linen was to be done by machine in a small building across the street from the café. However, I now had no place to sleep! Bunking out with a former girlfriend's family was just temporary as a favour to me. The cook at the café wanted to make a waitress out of me, but I was too shy to try that. Now what?

Prince George Hospital 1942

Well, I applied at the hospital and got a new job as a kitchen help, peeling vegetables, washing dishes and setting up meal trays. They were put in a hand-operated elevator up to the second floor and from there to each patient. After the meal, the trays were gathered and sent back down in the elevator. The ground floor patients had trays delivered by cart. The doctors and nurses had their own dining room. These tables had special dishes and silverware, serviettes rolled into each nurse's special napkin ring, and the silverware had to be placed precisely: forks on the left (a salad fork, dessert fork, and meat fork); knives on the right, blade must face the plate; spoons in order of usage, soup spoon at top, teaspoon in saucer, very formal. And all those dishes were washed separately. Breakfast time I liked because I loved grapefruit, and when I prepared the breakfast trays, the grapefruits had to be halved and the sections cut out as well. I would watch the cook, and when her back was turned, I would wolf down half a grapefruit. If caught, I would have lost my job! My salary included sharing a shack at the back of the hospital. The other person was a fellow employee who had a boyfriend who used to visit her and stay the night. I didn't know what caused the strange noises until much later. However, the shack soon was to be destroyed, so a room was obtained on the second floor in the main building of the hospital. This room was designated 'isolation' for people with contagious diseases, but I don't recall that it was ever used for that.

22 • Ida Nikkel (Humphrey) nee: Buchi

1943 - Marriage

The year was 1943. The Second World War was being fought, and the government was establishing an army camp and building an army hospital for the troops. In the meantime, the troops who were already based in Prince George were cared for in our hospital. My roommate was seeing a soldier, but one weekend had planned to go home to her local community. She asked me to watch for her friend. He would whistle and throw a pebble at the window. So when I heard this signal, I opened the window to deliver the message.

The soldier pondered for a moment then said, "How about if we go out?"

I thought about it for a moment too then said, "Okay." So we went for a walk downtown, stopped in the café for a coffee then went back to the hospital and made a date for another time soon.

It didn't take us long to decide to get engaged, but as the Canadian Army was fully operational overseas, and he was on a ten day furlough, we decided to get married before he was sent away. I wasn't eighteen yet, so had to get my parents' permission to marry. They approved of my soldier, so they did give permission, and it had to be in writing before the ceremony could be performed. Our wedding was simple. The ceremony was conducted by a justice of the peace at City Hall. I bought a new dress, one I could wear later and a pair of shoes to match. One of my girlfriends was my attendant, and one of the government employees was the second witness. The wedding over, we had an early supper at the café and went to the railway station to take the train to Toronto, his hometown. I was going to meet my in-laws for the first time!

We arrived in Toronto and took the transit to his parents' house. I wasn't greeted with any warmth, but neither was my husband! I learned later that the parents said I married for the army pay that a soldier's wife gets! (If the husband gives it to her!) After we returned from our honeymoon, we rented a shack since he no longer stayed in the barracks, being married now. He had work to do for the Medical Corp, ordering supplies for the hospital, which was being built for the soldiers already being taken care of in our hospital. Three months later, his troop was sent to military camp in Alberta, and within days they relocated to a camp in Manitoba then were sent to England and very soon to Europe. I went to the station to see the troops leave and cried all the way home.

We stand together waiting on the platform, knowing that the train will soon depart. I think, "Will I ever see you again?" While I try to hide from him my breaking heart. King and country calls, so he must leave. There are sergeant's stripes upon the sleeve of the uniform my husband wears with pride. Underneath my lowered lids tears begin to glide. Soon the waiting troops are urged to board and there's no time left to speak. "Goodbye" Is the anguished final word, devoid of any reassurance which I seek. The huffing puffing train has picked up speed, disappearing soon from sight. Blindly, on stumbling feet, I head for home while daylight fades into the coming night. I ask myself, "Will I ever see him again?". Painful weeks will pass before I learn to which army camp my husband has been based. Then very soon was transferred yet again, expanding war leads army to make haste! Each *transfer brought him closer to the war in a country hostile and unimaginably far. And every army wife who shares the pain asks herself, "Will I ever see him again?"* (From "A Soldiers' Wife" by Ida Nikkel, first published in the Prince George Citizen on the 11th November, 2009 and again on 10th November, 2015) I rarely received correspondence from him. When he was sent overseas, I quit my job at the hospital and went to Toronto.

My parents-in-law took me in and gave me a small room with a cot. I applied for a job at Toronto East General Hospital and was immediately accepted to work in their laundry, which was within walking distance. My supervisor there gave me the impression she resented me, but I didn't know why. So when I was offered the job of elevator operator, I grabbed it! The elevator was manual. I had to fling open the two doors at every stop on the trips to the sixth floor, and then I slammed them closed again on the return trips. This made my arm so sore at first. I wasn't sure I could keep on doing it, but I got so good at it. I stopped within an inch of the landing every time! I enjoyed that job and overheard many interesting conversations of the 'passengers.' I was prepared to stick with it however long it took for the war to end and the troops to come home, but was surprised by a job offer as an attendant at the information desk. I took it! This position was located on the main floor and included answering questions for visitors about patients and room numbers. There was a daily sheet with every patient's admittance or discharge recorded and general health concerns. Also included in my duties was signing for flowers or other gifts for a patient or ordering taxis for discharged patients.

Eventually the war ended. The troops were discharged and sent home 'alphabetically,' so my husband had to wait until the letter 'H' was eligible. He arrived home, one of the few who hadn't been wounded or killed. This city born and bred Toronto man while in the army had already decided he wanted to be a farmer. He loved the country and had met my parents, so he bought a used car, and we drove back to Prince George.

Adjoining my parents' farm was acreage that I had saved our money to buy. An abandoned building was on it that had been used as the residence for teachers when there was a school open. So we stayed at my parents' place while demolishing that and used the lumber to build our own two room house.

We hired a large piece of equipment to clear the land and started digging a well. We were almost down to water when there was a huge tree trunk covering the entire bottom of the hole. This made it impossible to dig further, so we continued to use the nearby creek for water. The house was heated with a wood-burning heater. The wood was obtained from the trees that had been felled to clear the lot. Now I discovered I was pregnant! Unfortunately, when I was about 5 months along, I developed pre-eclampsia and had convulsions. A rushed trip to the hospital resulted in an emergency caesarean, which involved being moved from the local hospital to the military hospital while the operating room was not yet fully equipped in either of them. (See Winnie (Warner) Russells' "A Nurse's Story" in *Life Before the Pulp Mills* by the Prince George Council of Seniors, ISBN 978-0-9738516-1-8) I survived, but the fetus was already deceased, and I was told I would never have a full-term or a healthy baby.

My husband had been working in a small local sawmill, as the army 'mustering out' pay had been spent on living expenses and building materials. At that time there were many small sawmills producing lumber and railroad ties as well, so if you were able bodied and willing to work hard, you had a job! However, when he borrowed my fathers' team to skid some logs, his inexperience resulted in the horses getting all tangled up and no logs were moved, and so the horses were returned before they got crippled! Then a major flood that came close to our place helped him decide that being a farmer wasn't his cup of tea after all. So we traded the farm to my brother for a 1941 Ford vehicle and drove back to Toronto.

To Toronto and Back

We drove to Toronto and rented a room from a family, and my husband applied for and got a job with Ontario Hydro. When we had saved enough for a down payment, we bought a small house that needed quite a lot of fixing. It was helpful that my husband was a handy carpenter and mechanically inclined, so we were comfortable and close to transportation and shopping.

Tyre Ave.

Now I was expecting a child again, and I was excited to find that we had fruit trees producing pears and apples, and we had healthy grape vines. Time goes by quickly, and soon we had a 3 year old son and were expecting another baby!

Leland

We lived in the west end of Toronto. The in-laws all lived in the east end, so we didn't do much visiting. In fact none of them ever came to our house! We got together once a year. The older sister made Christmas dinner, so we gathered there. The father-in-law had his own automobile fixing business. When he passed on from a long-standing heart condition, we were given a trailer that he used for hauling his home-made rowboat to a lake on the Trent Valley Canal. This was a two and a half to three hour drive north past Peterborough. We purchased a lot on the shore of Mud Lake and spent holidays and weekends gathering material to build a simple one room shack to add to the boat trailer while we saved enough money to build a proper cabin.

Mud Lake

The children and their cousins had so much fun fishing and exploring in the woods.

We took a side trip one day to launch our boat in the Trent Canal's hydraulic lift/lock. Large boats coming from the St. Lawrence River had to come through the lock, which was operated by opening the hydraulic front wall. The boat would float in the "tank" (lock) filled with water, and the boat would rise with it then drive out and continue on its journey. We shared the lock with a large boat that left very little space for our small craft! Sometimes we took the children to the airport, where they could watch a plane land or to a place where they could see a train chugging along.

I had no interest in driving, so if the car and driver wasn't home, I walked, took a bus or transit to appointments. If there was an appointment to which I couldn't take the youngest, (not yet in school) I would ask my neighbour. She was an older lady, and the boys called her Gramma Donald. They couldn't pronounce MacDonald easily! In Toronto, you never saw a pickup truck unless it was a delivery vehicle. There were only cars or public transit. One day I had to take a bus with our three year old, and suddenly in a loud voice he exclaimed, "Mom! Mom! A f---!" He was trying to say truck but had a pronounced lisp!

We never had enough money to feel free to make a visit back to Prince George to see my family or even to make phone calls, so it was a real pleasure when my parents made a trip to Toronto. We took them on an outing to Niagara Falls.

Niagara Falls

Niagara Falls with Leland, Sheldon and Dean

Then my sister Leona was old enough to want to experience something more than living at home, and since she had completed grade 10, she came to live with us. She applied and got a job at the Canadian Bank of Commerce close by. I felt totally jealous of her. She was good for the children. They loved her, but she was no help to me, not having been required to do housework at home. She didn't offer to help, and I didn't ask for kitchen help, so I encouraged her to go back home, and I've been ashamed of myself ever since! However, since she was homesick anyways, she accepted the bank's offer of a transfer back to their Prince George branch.

Keith

My husbands' health had been deteriorating, but I wasn't aware of it. He had no symptoms, except that he just wasn't working around the house like he'd always done. Instead he came home from work, lay down on the couch, and if the boys were noisy and wrestling, he would point a finger at each and say, "You sit there, and you sit there and don't get off until I tell you to!" After about 10 minutes, they would whisper to me, "Mom, can we get off?" And I had to say, "Did your dad say you could?" I never contradicted any orders, nor were mine ever contradicted.

One evening after supper, the two boys and their father were wrestling on the living room floor, which they often did, and then they went to bed. Later, when we were getting ready for bed, and I was checking the doors and turning off the lights, my husband said, "I don't feel good." He was having terrible chest pains. I phoned the doctor who said, "Get him to the hospital!" So I called the ambulance, woke up the oldest boy and told him to look after his brothers. I rode in the ambulance with him. He'd had a heart attack and was hospitalized for a month. Finally he insisted, "No more bed-pans!" He was determined to get up and go to the bathroom. When I came to visit that evening, he bragged about it, so pleased to have accomplished it. The next day he got to the bathroom but collapsed onto the floor on his way back to bed. The hospital phoned to tell me, but he was gone before I got there. There was no opportunity for a goodbye! The younger son felt guilty because of the wrestling they did the evening of his attack, to the point where I took him to have the doctor explain to him that it most certainly was not his fault!

So now, I'm a widow with four children to support. Ontario Hydro took care of all the costs and funeral arrangements, which consisted of a viewing and a cremation. We had discussed this years earlier, so I did not have to make the choice . However, his family was totally against this and disowned me for it! So I had no support except from his fellow employees, our lawyer and my mail carrier. When he realized the situation, he got my older son a job in the postal service working part-time only, but it helped him to use his free time for some outdoor occupation, and he also made some spending money. I could no longer give the kids an allowance. The insurance policy covered the mortgage and also a small cash payout .

I decided to learn to type, and maybe I could get an office job that way. Well, I hadn't learned the keyboard alphabet yet when I accidentally jammed the middle finger on my right hand. It bent 45 degrees and wouldn't straighten! I took a bus in the morning to the nearest clinic, where they put a plaster cast on it, and I was told to keep it dry for three weeks. When I went back to have the cast removed after another three or four days, the finger went back to its 45 degree angle. So I returned again to see what could be done. Now they froze my finger to insert a metal pin, like a two inch nail from fingertip to the knuckle in order to anchor it in the straight position. After a month the doctor was to remove the pin. No freezing this time! He pushed and pushed to try and grasp the pin with his pliers, but the skin had grown over the head of the pin due to the time lapse, and it was so painful I began to cry and shouted at the doctor, "My God. That hurts!" He actually looked surprised, but one more yank removed it. That didn't solve the problem with my finger. The tendon had snapped in the first place, and should have been sutured immediately after the injury. To this day the angle is permanent, and consequently, I cannot use my right hand to give someone 'the finger'!

So, now it was decision time again. My in-laws had disowned me, I had no job, and the last addition to my family was my one and a half year old son. My decision, finally, was to go back to Prince George. I contacted our lawyer. He was to arrange the sale of the house as well as look after the will, pension and so on. I started by selling the cottage and lake property, the boat and trailer, the car, tools, everything I couldn't use or take with me on the train. Our oldest son had purchased a second-hand motorbike with his money from the post office job, and wanted to ride it to Prince George, but I wasn't about to let this sixteen year old novice rider make that trip! So I arranged for the motorbike to be shipped by Canadian National Railway (CNR), and booked a compartment for us with our own bathroom and upper and lower bunks.

Meals were included. This was a holiday cruise, a pleasure trip to help me face the past and the unknown future. The train left Toronto in the late morning. We got a ride to the station with a friend I made while in hospital for the birth of our last son. She had a baby too, and we stayed in touch. The train trip was enjoyed by us all, and the children were so well-behaved that one lady who shared our table congratulated me on it!

To Rutland And Back

We arrived in Prince George very early in the morning, and my brother Fred and his wife Eva took the two older boys to their home while the two younger ones stayed with me, first at my parents' for a few days then with my brother Ivor and his wife Joan, who also had children the same age. Joan was a substitute teacher, and I looked after the children while she was working, all the while waiting for the money to arrive from the sale of the Toronto property. We soon found a house that I could afford the mortgage on and down payment. It was close to a school and within walking distance to shopping . It had a living room, dining room, kitchen, three bedrooms, a bathroom and a full basement with a separate entry.

Oak Street

Now I had to figure out how to make an income while staying at home to raise my children.

So I had a shower installed downstairs, and set up two bedrooms then I advertised for 'room and board' renters. The first one to come and check it out also brought his mother along to check me out! I thought he was eighteen, but he was only sixteen. I had pre-determined that I would not rent to middle aged men— only grown boys!' Within a week I had two more applications. One was a young man away from home for the first time with a job, and a Swiss immigrant who had a job at the local dairy. So now two of them had to share one of the basement bedrooms, and the fourth in an upstairs room that had been my three year old's, who now shared a room with me! That boarder left shortly because his job was transferred out of town. The only rule of the house which I

42 • Ida Nikkel (Humphrey) nee: Buchi

made clear to them all was, "If you get drunk and come home noisy and throw up, you'll only do it once. And after you clean it up, you're out!" I treated all the boarders like family, washed and mended their clothes, changed their bed linen, made breakfasts and dinners and packed the lunch boxes they took to work. One of them left to get married, and another one left because I was moving away. That's a story for later.

A few years passed, then we went on a family trip to the Okanagan, and the kids were so impressed they kept pestering me, "Mom, why don't we move to Kelowna? It's so nice there!" My neighbour across the back lane was a real estate salesman, so on impulse and out of curiosity, as I had no intention of selling, I asked him, "How much could I get for my house? The full price, no offers?" But I foolishly signed a contract, and the next day his prospective buyer came up with the full amount! I understood that a signed contract meant I had to sell. Now what? I cooked up a week's supply of meals to put in the freezer, left my two older kids in charge, and got on the bus to Kelowna to house hunt.

I stayed with my brother and sister-in-law, who along with my parents, had already moved to farm acreage there. A real estate lady drove me around, looking for something I could afford in an area suitable for my needs. I either wanted a place where I could run a room and board again, or one near a commercial area with transit close by, so I could find some kind of employment. After spending five days there I said, "No luck. I have to go back home tomorrow!" Well, she had one more place to show, a duplex with both sides rented. She didn't think I could get a mortgage since I had no income, only the money from the sale of my house! However, my mortgage was approved. So now I had to get back on the bus to Prince George to tell the boys to start packing, and to give away stuff that there was no room for in the moving van. My oldest son, Lee, drove the van, with myself and my youngest son, Keith, riding along. My son, Sheldon, had his own vehicle, and my son, Dean, rode with him. The tenants in my chosen half of the duplex had then vacated, so we moved right in. By this time all the three older boys had jobs of their own and places in Prince George, so they didn't want to move.

Once we settled in and Keith was enrolled in school, my next door neighbour suggested I apply for a job at a nearby motel as a chambermaid. There was no cooking involved, just more housework. I was hired, but it soon became apparent that the manager didn't like me, and I learned it wasn't actually my work that was at fault. She thought my sponsor, who was assistant manager, considered me a friend, and this was the rub! If you had another friend besides her, you were considered a traitor! I didn't need to be a competitor here, so I said nothing, and put up with the fault-finding, but I spent my spare time looking for another job.

The Sandman Hotel chain was being newly constructed. It was also within walking distance, and when I applied, I was accepted right away. This job included cleaning up the sawdust and bits and pieces the construction crews left behind, washing windows and installing drapes, putting shower curtains up, stocking the bathrooms with toilet paper, towels, water-glasses, face cloths, tiny samples of soaps and toothpaste, and setting up beds ready for occupants. One room at a time was opened for guests. This hotel was just across the street from a Sears store in a medium sized shopping mall, so I decided enough of housework. There must be other things in life. I located the Sears manager in charge of hiring to ask if any jobs were available. He checked and said, "No, not now", But I went back several times, and then one day he said, "They need somebody in the warehouse, shipping and receiving" So I applied immediately to the manager there, who gave me some papers to fill out, and I started my new job the next day.

It included opening and pricing a mountain of parcels. The price tags were printed on a little machine, from a roll of paper tape. (I made that machine, and still have the paperwork of appreciation). All the clothing that needed to be put on hangers was done by a designated crew of two or three girls. The hardware—tools, paint and such, was taken by hand-truck to the appropriate department. There was a lunch counter in the store, and the employees could buy their lunch from it or pack their own and eat in the warehouse. The job was only part-time for 24 hours a week, except at Christmas when it was busy enough to give part-time staff full time work. It was enough for me to manage financially because I had the rent money from the duplex as well.

After working there for a while, I had fun at the staff's very active Social Club, writing poetry: *The Marking Room The Marking Room is 'where it's at' without us there would be no merchandise out on the floor for customers to see. We open all the cartons, and sometimes this entails battle scars from staples, and broken fingernails. Now count and size and colour-code and stick the price tags on. Then do the whole thing over when you find the tickets gone. We admit we make mistakes (who doesn't?) once in a while, but when we do, you can be sure we make them with a smile! We'd like to have you meet the staff which constitutes the gears that turn the wheels of progress in the warehouse part of Sears: There's Carlee, who does parcel post (and other things, of course). Like all our other markers, she's a 'quality resource'! Who does division nine? (where mark-up is the game) Surely they all know by now the face and Lil's the name. There's royalty among us too...our Leah has been seen wearing the crown she earned as eleven's Corelle Queen. Princess Fran's a body who can sit in any chair and function most efficiently. Our royalty* is rare! Then we have an 'import' who when first she came, started in the fashion room. Jessie is her name. Marian and Julie do trucks (in warehouse terms) they handle paperwork and freight, and Saturday's returns. Ida's basic claim to fame is nylons, drapes and scanties. (where would division 18 be without their bras and panties?') Also The Ladies in the Fashion Room. The merchandise in 'Ladies Wear' is all hung up with loving care....Lucille, Barb, and Agnes do fashions.... if that's Greek to you, it means that they must first unpack then hang the garments on a rack. Plastic overwrap's a bore... removing it a shocking chore. Then there's pricing to be done. They take aim with fashion gun! Bring back empty hangers, then sort them out to use again. Empty hangers grab and bind...(there's a job to blow your mind!) And paperwork is nothing new. They get their share of this to do. This was written, so you'll know the girls that run the 'Fashion Show.'

The club held Christmas and other parties. During one Halloween party, another woman and I dressed up as devils. No one could guess who I was!

They had a bowling team too, which I joined but never made a decent score. But I loved best the singles dinner-dance group because that was where I met George Nikkel.

Our group had dined, and when the band started to play, those who already had a partner got up on the dance floor. Those who, like me, didn't have one, sat and waited and hoped!. Since it was a public hall and designated as a singles dance, there were a few single men there as well as our group. A nice looking gentleman came and asked me to dance, so we danced every dance! When it was over, every last one of our group had a ride home, except me!. So when George offered to drive me home, I gladly accepted. The ride was in a one-ton truck with a sort of cabin on the deck.

About two weeks later, I got a phone call. It was George asking me if we might go out for supper. I thought, why not? That was the beginning of the best years of the rest of my life! I assumed George was unattached, but we hadn't got into any personal explanations as to why or when. He didn't offer and I didn't ask, but my house was only three blocks from where he lived by himself in a two room shack. He invited me over to a barbeque, and then he made sure I knew he was divorced. He didn't go into detail, but he told me he had a teenage son, who lived with his mother. He also had a younger son who had perished several years earlier in a sandhill cave in.

We soon became serious. I was totally impressed by his consideration, his thoughtfulness and his talent. He was in the construction business and could do everything! Cement work, plumbing, wiring, roofing, he could do it all! Within the year, he asked me to marry him, and I didn't hesitate to say, yes. In the meantime, whenever he came to my house to visit, he would find something to fix. The first thing was an orchard ladder because I had fruit trees and a regular ladder was awkward to say the least.

Our wedding ceremony was by a justice of the peace, and for witnesses we had a married couple who were friends and neighbours to George for years. I bought a new dress, and George bought us all corsages. We had supper at a local restaurant, and George now moved into the duplex with me.

Wedding day

My paperboy had grown up, and was now a real estate salesman as well. He informed us that just down the street was a vacant lot for sale, so we went to look it over, and decided it was a very good place to build the house we had planned. Sell the duplex and build! So we did!

Kelowna

My job at Sears had changed into an on-call job. It wasn't worth keeping, so I quit after nearly fifteen years and became an apprentice carpenter. I loved it. I used to slow down and watch a construction crew as I walked to work. I wondered what they thought about onlookers. The house was my pride and joy. We would go to work on it in the morning, walk home to the duplex for lunch, and go back to work 'til dark! We moved in three months later, just in time for Christmas. There was still finishing work to do, but it had all the necessities: heat, electricity, water. The duplex had new tenants. The ad I placed in the paper said, 'No children, no pets' and was answered within days by a lady who came with her sister and asked, "Does that mean I can't bring my dog over when I come to visit?" I said, "No, it means no live-in dogs" Her husband was seldom home and moved away permanently soon after, and she became more a friend than just a tenant. I helped her with advice on gardening when she asked, as she always admired my small orchard, which I had started immediately. I had peach, cherry and apricot trees, a raspberry patch, rhubarb, grapevines and a walnut tree which we obtained as a tall transplant from a nursery. She helped me bring that home, although we could hardly get it into the trunk of her car! It stuck out so far we were afraid it might fall out! The root ball was so large it took a lot of digging to make a big enough hole to plant it in. And it didn't help that we had to pry a large rock out of the bottom of the hole when it was elbow deep. I hadn't expected that! Later on I added a plum tree and a kiwi plant. The kiwi actually provided some tiny fruits! The garden was small: a raised bed for cucumbers, green beans and carrots. I had only a few tomato plants because tomatoes were available in quantity and cheap from nearby farms. I still remember my very first taste of a tomato. It was at a lunch provided by someone, who had hired my dad for a job. The orchard also supplied us with apples by the pickup load. We made apple juice and wine, as George remodeled a washing machine to juice the apples. He also installed an underground sprinkling system in the lawn, so lawn watering was one chore I gladly could avoid. Summers in Kelowna were usually hot and dry. There wasn't anything he couldn't do!

We had a neighbour who used to come over and use the tools in George's workshop. This man wasn't too handy at complex projects, but made a nice bird house for me, which we attached to a tree up close and in front of my kitchen window. My sink was just below this window, and I enjoyed looking out while doing the dishes. One day I saw two sparrows fighting for possession of the birdhouse. They chased each other for a few minutes. Then one sat on the twig in front of the entrance, and was halfway in when the other bird flew over, grabbed a beakful of feathers and hauled it back out! They both landed on the ground below, mated and flew away, but the birdhouse wasn't occupied that summer.

I loved my life, the location of my home, the neighbourhood, my special home and good neighbours. There was, however, one thing that concerned me greatly, George's deteriorating health. His hard work over the years was catching up to his physical health. All the joints were wearing out, and in spite of the operations, there was endless pain, symptoms of heart and lung problems and high blood pressure. One day I voiced my concern. I said, "If I'm ever left alone again, I'm going back to Prince George." He replied with, "Why don't we do it now while we can do it together?" Well, I knew that he had never wished to go back to Prince George to live. He had lived there for years before settling in the Okanagan. He helped his brother, Bob, establish a business there, as well as completing many other construction projects. Anyway, he agreed for my sake, and so we started to plan our move.

First, we took a trip there to look for our new place of residence. After a superficial check of several houses, our real estate lady had prospects for us to consider. She knew that our finances didn't include mansions. However, she was also aware that George was a contractor with many years' experience, and had professional knowledge of renovating as well as working on new construction. As we drove slowly down the street, George was looking at this house, which prompted his verbal reaction to the sales lady. In a forceful tone of voice he said, "Keep driving, just keep driving!" My response was, "Please, let's check it out." This was because it was close to a bus stop, was within walking distance of a shopping mall and dental office, and the fact that he had the ability to do all the obviously necessary repairs and additions to make it presentable and liveable. It turned out to be a huge challenge. The following statement comes to mind: "making a silk purse out of a sow's ear." Our building was not just "a sow's ear," but "a pig's ass!" Definitely a fixer-upper starting with the roof! But I knew whatever else it needed, George could do it.

house before

So to humour me, we bought it, went back to Kelowna and put our home up for sale. Start packing again!

The first and most important packing truck contained the shop tools. There was a crude doghouse-sized building on the property to store them in. The biggest truck was loaded with metal strips of roofing material, the kind that locks together vertically with one and a half inch raised edges, and a special pliers-type tool. We had much needed, (and greatly appreciated) help for the moving job. A brother, one of the former neighbours and the sons, all filled their cars with boxes and bags, whatever could be stuffed in. It took several trips, including a truck load of second-hand glass panes for installing floor to ceiling windows in a large patio George added to the original house. First was the new roof, a major job to be sure! By now I had begun to wish I had agreed when he asked the real estate lady to keep driving. Altogether we relocated two entry doors, three inside doors, and closed in an open outside stairwell, which led to a half basement with a dirt floor. The water main shut-off was located in the crawl space! We eventually dug out the rest of the basement by opening a hole in the outside wall, and shoveling enough to allow George's engineered conveyor belt to work. He removed enough dirt, so he could rent and drive a small bobcat to remove the rest of it . Now treated timbers and lumber finished the walls, and a cement floor was poured. It was more of a major job than the roof had been! Every room had to have a new floor, new windows, new plaster on drywall and ceiling, new cupboards in the bedrooms and bathroom built or added to. As we both preferred oak wood, he built beautiful new cupboards of oak, and eventually the inside work turned the place into a home we were proud of! We learned that the house had been occupied by tenants, who changed regularly from one irresponsible family to another over the years.

After the house was liveable, George turned his thoughts to building a proper shop. First, he built a sawmill to produce lumber. Then he poured the cement floor. He built the shop which was large, wired, and insulated. Now back to the one remaining project on the house: tear off the old vinyl siding, make decorator posts for the newly added front porch and stucco it all! And, since I was still his only and best ever apprentice, it was only natural that I was going to learn stuccoing! He filled the wheelbarrow with the sand and stucco powder, added the proper amount of water and handed me the shovel to mix this plaster while he prepared the wall with the stucco wire.

house after

And so it went! We kept busy with woodworking projects, like building desks, bookcases, and shelves.

cabinet

I made flowers from some of the wood shavings.

flowers from wood shavings

(See vase in photo) Many passers-by stopped to comment on how nice the place looked now! I don't have peach trees and grapevines in my yard here in Prince George, but I do have a lot of apple trees, which produce more fruit than I can use, A couple of the trees I grew right from seeds. I also have a prolific cherry tree, a garden which will produce vegetables, strawberries, raspberries and a huckleberry patch which has spread into the far end of my one acre lot. It supplements but doesn't replace the annual hunt for huckleberries with my good friends, Regina and George!

Huckleberries

I like to try rooting shoots and sprouting seeds from all kinds of things, pears, plums, yams, cherries and pineapple tops. However, the walnut tree that produced five walnuts while we were in Kelowna, (that we brought with us and planted here) died down every winter and recovered in the spring. Finally I removed it because it was just too disappointing to keep trying!

The winters here are more severe and longer than in the Okanagan. They have four seasons, we have two! Except for a few weeks in the spring or fall, it's either summer or winter. You learn to adjust. There are moose, deer, and bear that regularly travel through the yard. One small bear was photographed by my neighbour, Roy. It was sitting on my clothesline stand!

Nearing the End

I have tried to adjust to a more devastating change of circumstance than just the weather. It's been over twelve years now since George passed away. He suffered a seizure while sitting in his special chair, a few feet away from mine. I heard him say, "I don't feel very good", and by the time I turned to look at him, he was gasping for air. I frantically dialed 911 and tried to position him, but couldn't with one hand holding the phone to give the operator our address. The ambulance arrived within a few minutes., The attendants administered shock treatment, resuscitation on the living room floor. Then they loaded him into the ambulance. My son had just arrived, and we followed to the hospital where they hooked him up with all the wires and tubes necessary to keep him alive. He was there for a week and seemed to be doing well, so well that he was able to laugh and joke with us when my daughter-in-law and I were visiting. Then two days later, a 2:30 am phone call from the hospital, "You'd better come immediately. George is not doing very good." By the time I called Leona and we got to the hospital, George was fighting like a wild man, trying to rip the tubes and wires out. It took the doctor, two attendants and myself to hold him down while another doctor injected him with anesthetics. He had stopped breathing and had no pulse. The doctor looked at me with an expression on his face that I read as, "Should we let him go?" In my heart I knew that George would not have wished to go through more of what he had suffered in the past weeks. I just nodded to the doctor and turned away.

It's been a long lonely time since that day, but I have wonderful caring neighbours, friends and family. I have everything I need to live financially secure, so that I don't have to penny pinch. I do, though. It's my nature to!

I was very young when I began expressing my thoughts and emotions by writing for birthdays, anniversaries, submissions to the Poetry Institute of Canada, Readers Digest and Our Canada, newspapers, newsletters, and two books mostly in poetic form, self-published as: *A Collection of Verse, ISBN 0-9734771-0-5* and *A Personal Collection, ISBN 978-09734771-1-5*

My youngest sister Leona, along with many others, try to fill a void I have lived with since my beloved George passed on. Now this autobiography, my *Road of Life* is an extension of my writings, and it is helping me to become published once again. The Road of My Life. How many more miles must I travel it? How I have wished it had been I that went instead! I know he is with me here in spirit. He proves this by the 'pennies from heaven' that he leads me to when I go walking, and the spirit writing that I have been doing for many years now. He will meet me at the beginning of the tunnel, Jesus will meet us at the other end with the light.

Ida Nikkel (Humphrey) was born Ida H. Buchi, October 5, 1925, in Prince George, BC, Canada. She grew up on a farm in the area, attended a one room rural school, and when she finished grade 8, she ventured out on her own. She met Alwyn Humphrey, a soldier from Toronto, who was posted to Prince George with the Army's Medical Corps. Married in 1943, they were raising four boys until his sudden death in 1966. She moved back to BC, supporting her family alone. While living in Kelowna, she met and married George Nikkel, and her road of life led her back to Prince George for some happy years until George passed away in 2004. She still lives independently, and loves to walk, garden, and grow plants and fruit trees in the summer. She writes poetry, stories, letters and knits up a storm of mittens, hats, socks and scarves. Here are her thoughts, snapshots and memories.

CPSIA information can be obtained
at www.ICGtesting.com
Printed in the USA
LVOW08s2027250617
539298LV00001B/15/P